A

History

of

Glass

A
History
of
Glass

poems

Bryan Walpert

STEPHEN F. AUSTIN STATE UNIVERSITY PRESS
2011

Copyright © 2011 Stephen F. Austin State University Press
All rights reserved.
Manufactured in the United States of America
Cover art: Harold Walpert

Stephen F. Austin State University Press
P.O. Box 13007, SFA Station
Nacogdoches, TX   75962-3007
sfapress@sfasu.edu

LIBRARY OF CONGRESS IN PUBLICATION DATA
Walpert, Bryan
A History of Glass / Bryan Walpert

p. cm.
ISBN: 978-1-936205-41-7

1. Poetry. 2. Walpert, Bryan

The paper used in this book meets the requirements of ANSI/NISO Z39.48-1992
(R1997) (Permanence of Paper)

For Nancy

ACKNOWLEDGEMENTS

Thanks are due to the editors of the following publications in which some of these poems, sometimes in different forms, first appeared or are forthcoming:

Bravado: "Closure"
        "Other People's Dreams"
        "Clouds Over Seattle"
        "Chicago Homes"
        "My Mother is an Onion"

Bryant Literary Review: "Thesis"

Buckle &: "Postcard"

Crab Orchard Review: "Improvisation"

Many Mountains Moving: "The Winemaker's Daughter"

Michigan Avenue Review: "How to Watch a Snowfall"

Mid-American Review: Thank You, Persia

The Modern Review: "Population: Two"

Off the Coast: "Sand" (from "Shorelines")

Runes: "In the Photograph"

Segue: "A History of Glass"
        "Aubade"

Tar River Poetry: "Cutting Onions"
"Mother, Reading"

"How to Watch a Snowfall" was reprinted in *Only Connect* (Cinnamon Press, UK, 2007).

"Apology" appeared in *The Infinity We Swim In* (New Zealand Poetry Society, 2007).

"Static" appeared in *2001: A Science Fiction Poetry Anthology* (Anamnesis Press).

"River Talk" is for Joel. "Rose, Dancing" is in memory of Rose Walpert. "Colors and Trees" is for my father. "Moment" is for Nancy.

Many thanks to those readers who offered feedback on this manuscript or on some of the poems: James Hoch, Michael Collier, Stanley Plumly, Tim Upperton, Jeff Dicken. Thanks to my parents, Harold and Naomi, for their support. Special thanks to my two children, Abby and Zach, for reminding me always what is important and, as ever, to Nancy Golubiewski for believing.

Contents

III.

ONE

Aubade

Smoke unrolled from their cigarettes
in patterns that wavered and shifted
like the topic of the talk they'd been
having all night, the one they'd
agreed they had long needed to have

about a relationship whose structure
seemed solid, like their intentions,
at the start but proved ethereal,
between them yet beyond either, as it
shifted and wavered until they agreed

to talk on that damp deck overlooking
the beach, and while she paused
to take a drag, he waited for her to finish
the sentence he wanted to interrupt to make
the long last point meant to undo all she said

he had done, the smoke meandering across
a moon whose pattern was as fixed as
his memory would be of that conversation
whose turns could not hide its turning
into the one with the usual subject,

a change one sees that the other does not,
or sees and does not wish to see
the other see, the one in which what was
unclear becomes as clear as the morning
promised the day would be along the line

of shore they'd left that deck to walk together
one last time as they spoke, or she did,
and to watch the waves roll, unroll,
arrive and slip away like something
that started as what they'd meant to say.

In the Photograph

that I have never seen,
the one my wife refuses to show me,
the one in the frame hugged to her chest,
she stands in a crowd, as I imagine it,
her hair larger, and looks ahead
to a future she has no idea includes me
imagining in the past
framed by this photograph a bird
sits just barely discernable in a tree
behind the voluminous mane of her head.
It has a red beak or, if the photograph,
which I might have mentioned I have not seen,
is black and white, it is a beak one might
have to imagine to imagine to be red.
I may be making too much of the beak.
The tree might be what most matters
in this photograph, the way its skeletal
branches importune something about
winter sneaking up behind her,
like the future she thinks
she's looking into, so young,
younger than I've ever known her.
It's a group shot, but the photographer
has noticed her. Not her hair,
which is beautiful, but the red line
of her lips, the smile he commands
darting too quickly across her face,
a bird alighting on a branch
then flurrying away, like the present,
as if noticing it has been noticed
by someone who wants to say to the person
beside him, Quick, look at that bird,

but that person will say, What bird? What tree?
Anyway, she'll say, this person beside him,
the person putting the frame face-down
on the table, then placing a book on top of it,
she'll say, Anyway, it's winter now,
and what's gone is gone.

Argument

We stop before it, the strange, quaking aspen,
its leaves a silent tremolo.
Like an old man who with each breath
rattles a little further from his life.
They say a single self, like a tone,
underlies the stalks in even a large stand.
Soon, you are stalking away.
The real matter, I know, is trust,
a hairline crack in its fragile surface:
I follow. *Are you thinking of her?*
The aspen trembles behind us.
It explains something of fear, so many
of one's parts open to the air, heir to winds
and blades, names carved, those silly hearts.
It is all about surface area, how much
we choose to show, how much is chosen for us,
like thoughts we are too late to hide—
sun-drenched skin of a bared limb.

The Common Names of Rocky Mountain Wildflowers

Fireweed ✧
(Epilobium angustifolium)

Ascendant
to be the sun
and light by rising,

to alight,
lips, for example,
on a cheek,
peaceful in sleep,
no hint of the anger

between us. When
you wake, we will,
as we always must,

repair what has been
undone. Some couples
must rise filled with light,

but one among us
must always
descend

to the history
of damage

to ignite a burnt field
with bloom.

Mountain Bluebells ✧
(Mertensia ciliata)

To touch
once
meant a bell striking,

tocare,
the music of skin
on skin.

How long now
have you and I
left one another
untouched?

You droop
as though
to drain your color.

To the leaves
our lot is sadness,

one minor note
if we wrap
ourselves around
we can almost feel.

Showy Daisy ✧
(Erigeron speciosus)

We grow old too soon.
Even as strawberries
ripen, we wither

and would rather
bare our faults
to the air.

Whose fault
is it now? What
message would you
send about me
to yourself
in the past?

Perhaps:

do not think
to bring those
home whose

call it is
to be unkempt,

ragged
even in bloom.

Moonflower ✦

(Mentzelia decapetala)

Our room is all air
and little luminescence,

a bare sheen
on your shoulder,

and still
I still my hand.

Like blossoming
shadows,

some open only

to light
reflected,

a cool touch,
distance.

Sun God ✧

(Hymenoxys grandiflora)

The way we promised
never to go to sleep

with distance between us
and then do. Each

in our thoughts,
separate ships,

we tack in parallel,

bow still to the east,
stillness a sail,

worship the slow
barge of light.

A Fugue

plays on the stereo
over the intermittent static
his steps make through snow
across the deck's warped boards,

the chords of the creaks,
those daily movements the boards
record, a cacophony pure
as the snow's uniform stutter

as it settled this morning, complex
as the purest fugue, the platonic ideal
of music, so ideal it is hard to hear
except in fits and starts, like the speech

or silences of an aphasic or a point
being made by someone with whom
he begins and ends each day,
a point he'd thought he had heard

until she asked *Weren't you listening
to a word I was saying?* and he admitted
he could not recall, which as past
is prologue meant that she would say

Why don't you ever listen, though he does,
sometimes, at other times poorly,
so when he asked her to repeat herself,
she would, out of a reasonable sense

of dignity, refuse because he had
proven again he could care less
what she has to say, even as he struggled
to recall her point from where it must

have crystallized in the rarified air
of some dendritic peak, recalled
the kitchen lit with morning brilliance,
her face as well. He had felt lucky,

but to tell her that would
of course meet with a disbelief
born of her certainty, albeit inaccurate,
that he felt obliged to say so, so

out of a truer, less nameable obligation,
he remained silent, as he is now,
the fugue rounding its last corner,
reminding him of a question someone

once asked: What happens to the notes
once they're played? If he could,
he would explain to that child, to that
version of himself, about vibration,

that all is formed from the sounds of strings
we can't see, that nothing exists of the past
in the present but footsteps, those he would
see circling around the back, past the bushes

covered with the morning-thought-thickness
of snow, those of a woman stalking
to her car, a second, larger pair scurrying
after, too late, their owner having stopped

for a missing boot, to put on a coat, to think,
might see in it a pattern, a recursion,
if he turned from the porch's not unpleasant
passivity, walked into the warm house,

climbed the stairs and glanced at the yard
through the upstairs window. The track
has ended. He stamps his feet,
sends up a small plume from his lips,

a fog of thoughts dispersed,
the snow started again
around him, poor, frozen, forgotten
notes toppling from their staffs.

Postcard

Things have not changed much. The objects around me have developed a sort of frost, so it's best to keep the window shut now. Anyway, it softens the sounds below, where along the boulevard the women sink neck-deep in their wigs, a hydrant releases a breath held since 1972. You could have guessed all this. The world moves at the pace of the sandwich bags scurrying in fits and starts along the curb. Meanwhile, the elm whisks a tentative SOS on my window, its leaves thoughts dropped absentmindedly. It continues this way without you, the way the manhole still sighs its shape into the cold air and so many watch-faces reflect until light rises from the street in many voices.

Just to Say

I came to that old poem,
folded in the leaf of a book,
and meant merely to take
a peek, like visiting a home

I'd lived a few years in long ago,
curious what had changed,
but of course it was the same,
and I couldn't help but linger

in that meadow where we still sat
as lovers. The air rippling through
the grass carried a thought
I could nearly catch

and still hushed the bees,
busy as always laying gold amid
the buds, while the sun slid,
endlessly of course, behind

cherry trees whose petals
fluttered like a feeling
I'd forgotten, as I'd forgotten
the scent of dusk that settled

along azaleas, the pond,
even the blanket somehow
that you had forever spread
beside the river for us to lie upon,

so it was only the foolishness
that seemed new, the kind
you feel when you find
you've come late to the obvious,

that even a first-time reader
should have known how soon
the end was approaching when
the jays, weaving shadow braids

between branches, sealed
the seam of the horizon,
descending to wherever it is
our oldest best selves are stored,

so forgive me if I've remained
too long in this poem. I'll leave
you asleep now by the river,
murmuring the memory of my name.

TWO

River Talk

We are sitting on the rocks.
You are rambling on about
catching fish in a moving river,
while I consider the clarity
of water before it wraps itself
like a gift, scattering small boats
of foam across its own surface.

Someday, I realize, someone will
look at a river in just this way.
An ancient Greek must have looked
in just this way, I think.
I am thinking his thoughts:
My goats wander the shore
somewhere, doing what they do;

someone plays what might be a lyre
while the river gurgles and gurgles.
Wait, that's you.
This is silly, you are saying. *You are
parroting the pastorals and have
no idea what an ancient Greek
might have thought.*

There is more from you,
but I am thinking of my goats,
of the sun's warm burden on my back,
of a woman. Her name is in Greek,
syllables I find with my tongue
unfolded like an old map. The trees
respond to the wind with an accent.
I notice you have one, too, still
chattering incessantly while I think,

though, no, this time it really is the river
spilling its language over the rocks,
challenging me to remember my name,
releasing its selves to the future
like whole caught moments.

Glassphalt Aubade

I spent one hot summer hauling steel
in a downtown warehouse, is what I tell people,
and though the summer part is true,
the heat, the warehouse downtown,

even the steel, I did precious little hauling.
Mostly I sat sweating (or maybe that should be
swearing—we did a lot of swearing,
what else was there to do) in my beard

and yellow shirt, sitting on a skid or stray
beam, wiping dust from my face, waiting
for the occasional order to lug a bar,
connect some joints, listening to the guy

talk about his spell in prison for robbing
a liquor store down one of the seventeen
streets Baltimore paved in part with crushed
recycled glass, which is just recycled sand,

which is just recycled cosmic dust
another guy liked to say over his lunch about
everything—it didn't matter what: bricks, steel, us—
all *cosmic dust* he said with his mouth full

of it, we said (or words to that effect)
—*no, I swear, I saw it on TV*—
the same glass streets reflecting the light
I saw while driving to work at six a.m.,

the roads glittering as they were meant to,
as we were all meant to, is what I think
the cosmic dust man meant, while the shadows
slid from the walls of factories like the blanket

peeled off a body that doesn't want to go
to work, wants to stay by the brook-like
babble of a cool dream, not come here to hear
the others laugh at the guy because he'd

been kicked out by his old lady, had cried like
a child, words hanging like the heat in the air,
like moments refusing to melt, as strong as the steel
that wouldn't be lugged, just sat on the shelves

staring back at us until the fat man slummed in
from his air-conditioned cubicle, trailing cold
like a cape, to tell us an order had come in,
meaning one of us would ride in the truck.

We stared at each other, then, sizing up our chances,
our minds on the snowball stand that seemed
to be on the way to wherever we were going,
a broken down shack, a wrecked ship of boards

on a sea of stone, the kid shoveling shaved ice
like diamonds into the white paper cone
—surely we were all thinking something
like that when the fat man pointed his bologna

sandwich at the chosen, who'd climb into the cab
of the truck, then stare through the side mirror
as the loading dock diminished from the entire world
to a door off the world, then disappeared,

the window rolled down, the cab filled
with the bad breath of buses, the stale farts
of factory steam, and I don't know about the others
but it poured over me like what they say

you search for at the bottom of a bottle,
a view of the world moving so fast around you
you might be forgiven for swearing
you were treading on stars.

The Mathematician

I slept in. You spent Sunday mornings
in the third grade learning points and lines from tutors
you soon surpassed. Even then you must have seen
square and circumference between legs of ladders leaned
against stone walls, in the sycamore shadows swept
by afternoon sun onto sidewalks, the way years later
you said circles chased you in cirrus clouds, in water
swirling down a drain, in sunlight early angled to your eye.

You remember last summer. You let yourself slip
below the surface of a lake. I spent a night outside,
in a meadow surrounded by stars even Einstein
could not express. Even he needed someone
to pack them into equations, to compress light
and time, as I did my tarp, once it dried of dew,
rolling the vinyl as if an expression of the air
and dark you had breathed and could no longer carry.

I'd dreamt of number strings drawn across a blackboard,
curved like night. Is this what you saw?
I understand. I could gaze beyond them, as through glass,
to see stars bend to gravity. I could see it clearly, as some see
circles on a page and hear the music so loud they must
shut their eyes to sit in silence, the way those of us stuck
at the surface of slate or sheets, as I was when I awoke,
draw a shade on Sundays to catch some sleep.

Other People's Dreams

Each night you enter: by a door
to the woman you spoke with yesterday
on a balcony, onto a train with a man
you haven't seen in the days
or decades that pass like darkness
in the deeper hours. They must,
some nights, draw you wrong:
nose too broad, eyes aquiline,
but, mainly, the words:
in soliloquies of single syllables
you would never in sunlight say,
you betray yourself, disrobe
in hallways, commit acts behind
the eyes of a neighbor, a cashier,
the driver of the number six you rode
as a school child: as moonlight
hums unheard behind a curtain,
you ride a bus up a hill to the home
of someone else's childhood,
slip off socks, stroke a thigh,
nod *yes, yes,* to thoughts that shed
their suits and sing to one another, softly,
behind walls, so as not to wake you.

Closure

The click confirming
your diary's closure
then the slide of the rollers

as I shut your dresser drawer
and click off the light
bring to mind the sensual swivel

at a safe or the daring risk of a latch
on our screen in early summer,
less true barrier than suggestion

of boundary and border,
the rebellion of its mesh
a kind of permission for the snarl

of a stranger's mower or
the smoke of his cigarette
to wander as at will into the house

and caress with scent your skin
as you prepare lunch for our children.
How much we entrust to the slip of bolt—

a locked house to a deed as a mind
to a thought. Consider all the crannies,
how many forgotten keys to forgotten

doors lie abandoned but waiting
to be rediscovered, like the secrets
they embody, as in symbol,

in dresser drawers, shoe boxes.
I say bless the scrape of the glass door
to the jeweler's cabinet, the death rattle

of the janitor's keys, the prim jingle
of those encircling the virginal wrist
of the blond bank teller. Keys imply

the prowler, the trespasser, the unchaste,
who refuse to accept an answer, while
dangling the unknown, the behind,

that expanse of what is not yet but will be
wished for. How tempting the hook
of a bra, the fumble of a button,

the bewildering way a barrier beckons.
How sweet the refusal of a door,
those things we think we want

which appear merely to hover
just above the day or just beyond
the impassive eye of a lock, or lover.

The Glass Blower

At some point it occurred to him
how funny it was. It was fragility
that drew him into this business,
not just of the substance itself,
how it might shatter, as a shout
from a far shore can split
the afternoon, but how frangible
the moment of creation, how it,
too, could burst, had to be handled
like a lady, is how his first teacher
had put it, a man of the old school,
which even as an apprentice struck
him as an unlikely way to describe
a woman. Yet that is what he had found.
He was the kind unaccustomed
to any sort of amorous attention,
felt flattered that she lingered
by his lehr to look at his equipment,
to marvel at his metal table, that she
seemed genuinely impressed with
the way he'd wield the iron tube
of his blowpipe. Which bespoke,
he knew, why he spoke with her
as though she too were breakable,
which she seemed to want from him:
he knew enough to know a light
touch was required, a steady hand.
Even when both were bathed
in perspiration, it was understood
they were not to talk about it, only
around it, as carefully as they attended
their very motions late at night

in the dim studio so they would
not draw any of his pieces to plunge
itself over an edge and emerge
changed. Theirs was a language
less than liquid, an ardor always
annealing. Kneeling before him,
she seemed always on the verge
of irreparable damage. He was gentle.
He knew it was this, the source of his
greatest regret, that gathered her to him.
This is what they had made. He could
not change its shape, could not bring
himself to break it off. Even like this,
in flagrante delicto, she needed her caressing
carefully considered, fucking delicate.

Thank You, Persia

You're sorting through the useless crap
   that flows through the front door.
      Never mind why, you have a job to do:

gifts sent free in the mail, perfume
   sample, one-serve shampoo, all the free stuff:
      key chains, stickers, throw-away camera,

mini picture frames, the birthday gift from someone
   who says, *Oh, he'd never buy himself that*, though
      maybe you did say you like cows, might be your

fault on every occasion there is a grin fit
   to burst the banks of the gift-giver's face:
      a ceramic cow statuette or cow mug or cow calendar

or cow clock, the one where the animal makes
   an unlikely leap over a celestial object.
      And the poems that arrive in the mail, slipped

under a door, tucked into a bag. Oh, you appreciate them,
   every one, even if it is the third time you've received
      this particular translation of some half-baked bard

from ancient Persia going on about lute this or goat that.
   Though you're guilty, too, aren't you? Your friend
      liked shot glasses embossed with the names of the states,

so when you'd fly on business you'd pick one up
   for him at the airport—this is before you'd thought
      as carefully on this subject—and it was around

Minnesota that his wife took you aside
   and did you a favor. Then one day you find yourself
      reading that passage where the shepherd boy

abandons his goats to play his lute by the river beneath
   the brightest moon in Persia, a moon balanced like an egg
      on his palm, and who on his way home fills his bucket

with what turns out to be (you'd forgotten this) pure light,
   and setting aside for a minute what impure light
      might be, the purity of that light is so clear,

so indescribably clear—you've never noticed
   how good this translator is—it reminds you
      of the face of your friend's wife when she

married your friend at a ceremony in a meadow,
   the reds and yellows of the wildflowers so vibrant,
      the sun so bright, you had to rub your eyes to make sure

you were awake. She looked up at your friend
   in the purity of that light, and this is before
      he'd fill his shot glasses, lined up along

the coffee table nearly every night, before
   the late night phone calls to ex-girlfriends,
      before the light drained from her face

the way it slid behind the hills the evening
   they were married, first the colors of the wildflowers
      giving notice, then the hills, finally the color

of the sky slipping from the party for a rendezvous
   with day on the other side of the earth, maybe where Persia
      used to be, since even there a shepherd must wake

to the musical bleating of his flock and be grateful
    for this sudden gift of light, which makes your friend
        an idiot for holding up his shot glass to look through

the thick amber at his wife, a stranger, makes
    you grateful for every stupid gift, though you
        would trade it all in for someone to look

at you as she did at him, just once, someone
    to shepherd you and all your useless crap—your
        key chains and mason jars, your tendency to be critical

of others because you see in them yourself—
    from one difficult day to the next, to wake
        to your bleating in the dark, to tell you the sun will rise,

to hand you a poem someone has slipped under the door
    that contains only one word over and over,
        your cow-shaped clock ticking, its tail swishing

the seconds, which is where you come in,
    where you walk downstairs to sort through all the key chains
        and egg slicers, where you take it all, all the crap

you've accumulated over the years—the guilt and regret,
    the resentment and righteous indignation—
        take it all to the garage, throw it in the trunk, drive

past the meadow and the wildflowers, then dump it all
    in the river, even sell your car, maybe not today
        but soon, then walk, as the streetlights shudder to life,

you walk through the shortest, coldest days to where
    you're going, to the moon, to Persia, it doesn't matter,
        the trip is free, all you've got.

Clouds Over Seattle

Not wisps or dreams, but a high form
of fog the nose of this plane slices

through, toward you, my destination,
grounded in your certainty

my head is in them too often,
a trip become too familiar.

You may be right: Who are we
to knit space with something as sharp

as desire? We wondered
aloud once what the moon was.

It was all of those things,
though our arrival turned it to craters

and dust, so solid and sure we've
had to turn and stare back for wonder

through space at what we are in
the darkness: a drop of blue behind

trails and puffs that now and again
gather to descend as what sustains us.

Improvisation

To shoot the album cover
for *Jazz On The Beach*
required four men to not
exactly play jazz but
to appear as if they played
jazz on a beach, December
waves frozen like their
breaths against a gray sky
the mind sees as blue,
though the photo is black
and white, its frame cropped
against the moment before
the moment captured
to capture sound or the eye
of the ear that will hear it,
an instant that slips back
among the others as the tide's
tongue slips unremembered
into the mouth of the Atlantic
in New Jersey behind men whose
sand-scratched trumpet, bass,
and drums would carry scarcely
a whisper over the static
of the sea, would not make
it more than a few steps
down the sand that stretches
even further into the past
than music, if they played
to anything but the camera,
played anything at all:
a moment of pure sadness,
of being alone, adrift on such

moments, notes floating over
the drive home, the stoplights,
a quartet on the radio, dinner,
stretching for sleep, which
waits with the patience of sand,
one grain so like another,
a moment that has eroded us.
There, we've done it again.

Cutting Onions

The strength of its scent
stops you, the way a hand might
or the bad news in a letter

unfolded down the hall,
its sheets stained with the same
scent still hovering in high

corners of the bedroom,
poised to roll down walls,
travel the lamplight

onto your sweaters. You squeeze
your eyes to the dripping that picks
up speed outside as a patter

through the kitchen window,
a spatter of droplets through
the screen, onto the floor,

until you are wading through
memories, layered like her skin
freed into the household dust

that floats and gathers the way
thoughts do, randomly, of a salad,
how she taught you to make one,

as you do now: quick incisions
in the skin, the scent released
and rising from the slice,

an unraveling, a lack of depth,
a certain sameness, the weather's
alteration, steady and slow,

the rhythm on the roof,
a dissipation of air
so thick you could hide in it.

Thesis

Consider the certain rhetoric of flatware.
The drawer's slots, the clean classification:
A knife's urgent appeal to pathos—
it points to the heart.
The teaspoon's quiet humor,
hint of sugar to cut the truth.
Like any good counter-argument,
the soup spoon reflects its examiner,
albeit in distorted fashion,
tongue and teeth.
Even inch-deep into the flesh,
each greasy tine of the fork makes a claim
for civilization, offers its statuette to ethos:
We are who we say we are, our hands clean.

The Winemaker's Daughter

All autumn I have Father's blood
on my hands, my arms and calves
and neck, these purple bruises,
and even when he does not
keep me here on the hills,
in the fields, as he does more
and more as I come into my fullness,
covered like shame by the leaves,
or shivering on the cold floor
of the factory, as the machine licks
and slaps the labels on the curved
bodies of the dark bottles,
there is no way to hide to whom
I belong, as I wish to do
when I see the boy in town.
I can tell he would prefer me
pale as a fresh cake of soap,
so I rinse in the irrigation spouts,
in the pond behind the house,
in the basin in my room,
while Father's dog follows me,
follows me, his filthy paws
scratching against the wood floor
until I kick him away,
let the water trickle down
my face, my throat, over
the tendrils of hair that creep
down the back of my neck,
and for a moment I forget.
Each new grape is an ache,
a thought breaking into being.
I would let them die on the vine.

I would rather lie here on my bed,
imagining the boy as my lover;
it is he climbing the trellis,
slithering through the window,
he licking the ink
from even the arches of my feet,
his warm tongue I can feel
even now slide its hunger up my calf.
That dog, that dog. Out,
out damn Spot.

My Mother is an Onion

I spend the day reading student poems
with this title. One student's mother
leaves a bad taste in his mouth; another's
gives the soup of her life its savor;
a third discovers layer by layer within
herself, as she ages, the seeds of her mother's
own frustrated desires; and one mother
brings her son so often to tears that he must
keep her in the dark of a psychological
root cellar. I'm supposed to assign grades
but put it off, gaze through the window
by my desk as shadows stretch in the yard,
light blossoms behind the oak. I feel
I should instruct them to learn something
about the onion. I should tell them
Egyptians once worshipped it for markings
of eternity in its spherical shape,
its concentric rings, which are so much like
the circles we travel: my sister and I
around our mother, my daughter
and I around hers, my own around
my grandmother, a month in the earth,
my mother ten thousand miles away
in the privacy of her mourning. I wonder
what she is doing now. Probably,
she has been asleep for hours on the other side
of the world. Probably she's wondered why
I haven't written a poem about her lately,
about the care with which she has tended the year's
vegetable garden. She would want me to be
true, as she always has, to the observed world:
sweat in the folds of her neck, dirt

beneath her nails, but she would want me
to move beyond such descriptions,
not to suggest that she, too, has come through
the darkness, a moderate freeze or two,
but to find in the world some corollary
for how we all want to be compared
with what is pure, beautiful, rare,
to suggest we, too, are worthy
of worship, the kind our children offer
before taking it away. What I know
of my mother seems suddenly
tendril, for there is no vegetable garden
to sow, only houseplants on the balcony,
hanging like questions.
Yet I think my mother would allow it,
would say, *you are still young, it is not too late,*
and though I have no more idea than you do
what she means or to what spectral shed
she returns tools she does not own,
I promise you she picks them up from the grass,
and before leaving the poem for the dream,
of the future or the past, from which I have
so selfishly summoned her, she stares now
with me toward that unreachable distance
into which the day goes to seed after seed.

THREE

A History of Glass

The sound is a dull throb. Make
that sharp. Can a throb be sharp?
It is like a beak
through the brain, like he is
crafting his own image in sound.
I should kill him. Nearly have,

every morning.
Think of the axe in the garage.
The chickens would miss him.
Sentimentality,

says my friend,
who has both chickens and children.
We're at a party, on the deck, the light
wobbling, sinking over the hill.

I'd kill him,
the rooster, I mean,
but I forget during the day,
it fades, becomes memory of
memory, like they say
about childbirth. Try
to hold a memory of pain.

Here's one:
body against glass.

Don't like that one?
Return to the rooster,
a fucker

called Victor. I didn't
name him, but it sure
makes killing harder.
Names, I mean.

I don't mean
for the children we're still
trying to conceive.
How did we get onto children?
Can a throb be sharp?
A man buys a house,

inherits chickens,
didn't ask for them,
but accidents happen:
A man walking
across a street, late, toward
early morning, a black shirt

like he is not there,
then is, against the glass.
Then isn't.
Fault is just philosophy.
They wouldn't give me the name.

Just the image, then: a man
on the ground by my car,
breathing. Heavy,
like he is trying to catch
his own body.

Sometimes, the image
of his voice breaks into
a dream. Victor's voice, the rooster's.
Someone starts to scream, but I wake

to the crow before my brain
can weave a narrative.
Some stories don't want to be told.
Not a sound from his mouth.
Just a thud against glass. Though
the brain wants to add texture,
imagine distances,
movement, voice, blood.

Some people do it
without trying. How?
Children, I mean, happy accidents.
They're meant to be eaten,

says my friend (meaning chickens),
pointing with his third bottle
of beer, the party alight
beneath the stars, the other bottles
clinking at his feet, glass,

a supercooled liquid
that lets in light
and sound. Close the window
against the cold and still
hear the call of first light.
A history of glass

is sand and lime,
narrative of containment. To see
but not feel. To hear a little.
A lattice of lines spreading
layers of street light.

I inherited the axe
and its narrative,
clean, but not spotless,
I imagine. When
you have children,

what do you tell them
about what you've done
and what do you leave out?
It's like any story. My friend

tells me to kill the bird
or I can hire someone.
I'd rather do it myself.
Or feel I should rather.
I'll do it tomorrow
or Monday.

It's easy, he says,
dropping his arm in pantomime,
a swift motion in the dark.

Apology

If you could you would
bathe me in it, this (hell,
I will say it) love
that chases all shadows
from the room but yours.
Brilliant. Oh,
there are hard places
to reach: an angle behind
the far corner of the desk,
the inner tip of my shoe,
that swath of rug beneath
the thickness of a door,
places one might not think
to look. I know them,
could map them like the spaces
between constellations. O,
when we met, you asked
what I was like. I should
have told you I kept
night in my pockets.

Population: Two

You probably meant to hide out there
for an hour, wouldn't want me to see
the way you stare at the skyline,
as though mentally dismantling
the bank tower, bakery, post offices.

Are you wondering whether it is too late to dismantle
what we have built without our even knowing the design
until intention is revealed not just in its structure
but in every structure that composes it?

Just a guess. Look at the mountains,
how they compose the dusk, the script of history,
is what I would tell you, were we speaking.
Look at the puddles of pale silence,
spilled like old milk, like weak wattage
from the bedside lamp. Imagine a clay
that vanishes, leaving the abstract design
of structure, the outline of an idea.

What we have built can still be seen
as the glimmer of a ghost town
at the moment of waking or when given
shape by the sound of a train, which cuts
like a kettle's whistle through an unpleasant thought.

Look over your shoulder.
The deck's sliding door is open.
I'm watching you
watch the long-dead stars still
shouting their message in light:
Remember us. Remember us.

Static

What could they have thought:
Arno Penzias and Robert Wilson,
working in innocence in 1965
for Bell Telephone,

hearing again and again through headphones
a hissing like an old-fashioned
wax cylinder their
grandmothers

might have used to entice violins
from the afternoon air
of a living room,
and confused,

checking and rechecking their equipment,
even climbing into their
satellite dish
to sweep out

the bird shit, unable to escape the sound
that swept through their
speakers, then
discovering

they had found proof of the first explosion,
the one that set us in motion:
stars spinning, the earth
emerging

from the sun's gasses as a ball so tiny
that a girl I might have met,
if my grandparents
hadn't sailed

from there, could reach across water
to touch me as I sit here
in afternoon light,
reading

that the universe might one day fold in
on itself, and waiting
for someone
to call.

If a wait is, as some say, a lifetime,
then that ring, whether it reveals
what I fear or hope
or nothing at all,

will end me in a way whose arrival
is merely an estimate,
like that of winter
on my window,

crystalline dust which, if it were heated
beyond water and gas, if it
could get hot enough,
would split

into the unseen strings whose vibrations
(my book says) sing the full moon,
my birch, the bookcase,
the entire

world at a pitch that can be touched,
and would, physicists say, reveal
itself as the reverse of
the Big Bang,

one I've searched for all my life, recalling
a future whose signature still sounds
as background noise:
the music

of the stars expanding space like an ocean
stretching up the shore, or the noise
that seeps from the next room
as I try

to listen long distance, or the kind
in the receiver itself when wires
cross: a stranger speaking,
something Slavic,

a tongue that strums the air of my ear
like someone I knew once
or would want to,
or wait for.

Mother, Reading

He knew you had the mind because he watched you devour
an encyclopedia set he'd bought you, volume after volume

beneath your school desk or at the kitchen table while he
attempted to deliver a scolding to your down-turned eyes,

the ruffle of the flipping pages when he took a breath.
Your father insisted you could never become a nurse

because you were *too hard*, he told your mother,
recalling how at seven years old you had jerked your hand

from his to cross among the cars on your own.
Still, when the psychologist warned *Don't break her spirit*,

your father released his hand from yours, a sweep
of a gesture, a man opening a cage door and stepping aside.

A quarter century later he lay on a cot in his coma,
nine weeks of I.V. drip like a clock ticking in your mother's

dining room, an occasional yawn that made me, at ten,
dream again and again that he'd wake as if from a nap.

You changed his diaper, rolled his body, wiped the sweat
that rose like dew each morning from his forehead,

listened for a pause in his breathing until you found one
and came to tell me, as I sat on the backyard swings,

that my grandfather had died; you didn't hide it.
Then you walked inside to wash your hands and pick up

a book, the way when he'd yell at you as a child—
you had woken him or had broken the shabbas—

you'd lower your eyes to the page, as if you were alone.

Rose, Dancing

The Sunday you died, I attended a concert
in the park. They played "Sing, Sing, Sing"
as a finale while I stared into the trees,
back against the blanket, recalling
how you'd loved to dance, insisting the boys
who'd pursued you when you were young
found you *lively*, you said, not the beauty
the wedding photograph shows you to have been.
More than sixty years of marriage, though
in the five since your husband entered the earth
you dwindled like the last evening light
did as the concert came to a close
amid the gathering of jackets and bags.
The concluding concert of the season,
a sigh at the long end of summer,
when they played that song, I recalled
the story you'd told me again and again:
your first days as a wife, my grandfather
arriving to find you jitterbugging
alone in the living room, moving
like a moth before the open windows.
I wish I'd thought to ask the tune,
if you even remembered, but I do know
he asks *What will the neighbors think?*
before lifting the phonograph needle
then closing all the curtains to keep you
to himself. Even when the tune had ended,
when we'd worked our way to our cars,
flipped on headlights, returned
to our lives, I imagined you cutting a rug
alone between the wars, Victrola
at full volume, your husband heading home.

Another woman might have resisted, I suppose.
But you were *married*, you would have said
again, which mattered more to you than the music
ending, the drapes drawn around you and your husband,
descended together to the end of day.

"Colors and Trees"

The road is empty, as though I've arrived
a moment late, as though had I come
to this painting earlier, had I not stopped

for breakfast or to walk around the lake,
I might have seen someone just passed
on the road winding past trees that are

not maples, no, nor elms nor any species
you tended in that distant backyard
of my childhood, none at least that I

can identify, perhaps because you've
drawn them—strangely—blue,
blurred against the sky, as though seen

by someone focusing elsewhere. You?
Me? While you're taking questions,
where might that road lead, if anywhere,

if I turn it, as seems apt at this point,
to symbol? The time I thought symbol
redundant to sufficiency—that is,

that things suggest themselves—has gone.
I've never asked your opinion. Still,
and at considerable risk of sentimentality,

shall I guess the road you've painted to be,
as seems inevitable, your journey or mine
as you see it, or is it wishful thinking

that you'd have been thinking of me,
of the prospect it was I who'd passed,
you who'd missed me by a moment

whose length you have measured as a gaze,
so that you have granted me (yourself?)
the moment before my arrival? In asking,

have I become the artist, you the audience,
so I might return it to you, place you beneath
a canopy of color you probably believe

you have little time to spare to see
on your way beyond the picture's far curve?
Though what of the branches arched

over the road, touching like hands,
of course, but whose, and whose decision
are we talking about now, yours or mine,

creator and created both? Are you reaching
to me, or am I, in creating this picture
of your reaching, reaching? There is nothing

on the road, your having gone, just me,
commenting to no one on the curious colors
of the trees at precisely the moment we're passing.

Moment

From the same root as movement,
it settled into an instant,
enough to move the pointer of a scale,
as a feather might, or a petal

from the sunflower you gave me that summer.
Its long neck curved from your hand
as if staring at itself in the gloss
of my floor, a pond grown suddenly solid,

and that afternoon, my car parked
and sunk into wet grass and mud,
we trembled on a Ferris wheel frozen
over the earth, swinging in the wind,

excuse enough, nearly, to hold on
to each other. We didn't know how long
the moment (from momentous, a mark
of grandeur and importance) would last,

and how could we have then?
A minute is consistent, a sixtieth
of a circle, but a moment
does not warn of its departure

so we might know when to hold one,
when to wait one or when,
as the ticket man told us, the ride's
over, kids, time to move on.

"Chicago Homes"

In your painting, there are two, the same
light in both sets of windows, the moon
above them a halo, though misshapen,
though the whole scene wobbles
like a reflection in water. It's cold,
clearly, each shape exhalation, a cloud
emerging in naked brushstrokes like a child's

picture of afternoon, like the history
of a thought pulled from the depths
of a canvas or placed, like a sculpture
of two hands, as in prayer, in the corner
of a room. The past is an ocean of hands,
one of mine raised to ask a question
about history. Foolish question: the moon

looks over a cold pair of homes that stare
as if into the future, as if alone, like us,
living like neighbors, our past a set
of rooms masquerading as thoughts.
History hides itself in us, the way water
masquerades as the sea. Each afternoon
is a kind of sea, its familiar background buzz

the silence of one word drawn across history,
what we take to be emptiness. Some days
I walk home, or, if it's cold, I run, afraid,
through the fog. Think of thought as a kind
of cloud you disperse with a question
of breath. Some days, each exhalation is a stroke
of luck, each past an etching in a frame,

unbrushed dust. Sometimes windows
are just windows and before them,
some evenings, we share for one moment
one memory carved from the air,
the way figures emerge from a sea
of stone, half-naked, half-
formed of their own rooms.

Shorelines

Catch

a blue crab, the size
of two cupped hands. Boil. Break

off each limb. The stars become
visible: lung, language to settle
into constellation. Pull

the tab on its belly. If the shell
splits sharply, you may cut

your hands. Inside
is the world seen through

cupped hands. Sky
the odor of salt. The jagged outlines
of this world. The crab

has become your hands. They
carry the world below

you. Crawl
to bed inside of them.

Beach

your body on the bed. Its
linens are stiff

as wind. Dive.
The window rattles,

the springs creak. Wind
the sheets around

you, a river lining
the long bank

of the wall. Unfold
the blanket

of your body. Be sure.

Shell

peas into the sink, peer
through the glass

into the yard. Remove
a clam like a heart

from its body, lifting your hand
like a bird, a body

at one. The light hands
itself to you, whole,

an egg in your palm. Lift
to your ear like the sound

of the spray. A mile away.
Stand on shore alone. August
is a tone.

Float

a skiff on your easel. Cut
the paint. Deep

down, you are the color.
It is getting

cooler. The dusk grows
deeper. Soon it will determine

the horizon. You could
deepen the color. The tide

rising. Make waves
with a razor. Skip it. It's easy.

Sand

the gray deck, scattered with
holes through which the light

drains. Smooth its rippled
surface. Stand, stare at the shore

lined against an horizon leaking
day. Listen,

you have to come in. The rain
will slick our surface. Listen,

together, scattered, infinite
are we

How to Watch a Snowfall

Turn off the television,

the telephone,

douse the overhead,

every other

lamp, my love,

any electric

buzzing above

the buffeting

wind that wends

through our window.

Forget its faulty

frame is one failure

among many

we've managed

to fail to fix.

For now, follow

the snow

settling to slant

(nothing in love

or nature knows

a straight line)

along streetlights

to paper the ground,

a print-hungry page,

a world waiting

for words,

though don't deliver:

let them dissipate

slowly from our

saliva as steam,

as the breaths

we become

until our

thoughts tap

the ashen earth

in tandem

with every flake

and fall fresh

with every inhale,

exhale,

slicing, sure

as a caesura,

moment from

moment,

crystals

collecting in corners,

the hour

arriving

at its emptiest,

our entrance

into the instant

        as air,

as the glow

        of winter glass,

as snow itself

        tumbling toward

sidewalk and street,

        gathering speed

like a sentence

        that should

someone speak,

        we'd shatter.

Class Discussion

First snow falls
on the half-finished bridge.
                    -Basho

All afternoon snow falls, as on
Basho's half-finished bridge. Light falls
through the half-opened blinds
onto the table, over which this poem
is disputed. Why does it seem
suddenly so difficult to me?
Perhaps the speaker is approaching
middle age, someone suggests,
so all things seem elusive.
Yes, another says, the snow
is the first hint of white
in the speaker's hair, which
he has arranged in a comb-over.
I touch the top of my head.
And why *falls*, asks a woman,
her eyes closed in emphasis,
her head thrown back, as if
she planned to stick out her
tongue to catch the flakes,
so young she would not think
twice about a world arranged
to suit her taste: Why not just
have it all already sitting there
for the speaker to come upon:
the crest of a long hill,
snow covering the valley, ice lightly
on the river, from which only some

wood pylons, a few boards, extend
as the speaker stops to compose
himself. There is some place he had
hoped to reach, perhaps someone,
but even as the words
he had planned form in his mind,
as he writes them into the lines
of the landscape they slip
like scent into the cold air,
and anyway he is struck
by the beauty of the blossoms
of snow on his boots, or rather their
wabi-sabi, their imperfect beauty,
for even as he notices them
the vibrations of his steps
have settled the flakes into
less and no less satisfactory
patterns. He knows nothing
is less satisfying than resolution,
than having, something that now
seems only an idea, like the future
into which I like to think he will turn,
unbothered by disappointment
or anticipation, towards home,
where someone will be glad
to see him. Perhaps as he
approaches he will see smoke
from his own chimney etched
across the sky, which soon
will darken, as he sits by the fire,
the objects of his life arranged
around him, a sky from the greater
perspective of which one might
see students, the class over,
having smoked beneath the balcony,

one by one braving the weather,
the ghostly blossoms of their
breaths merging with the snow,
drifting to other buildings
or cars or the middle distance
into which this afternoon extends,
nearly complete.

CPSIA information can be obtained at www.ICGtesting.com
Printed in the USA
LVOW100219300112

266109LV00003B/3/P